Have You Gotten A

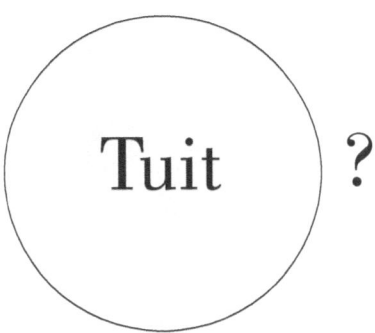

(Tuit)?

The Little Beige Book

Have You Gotten A

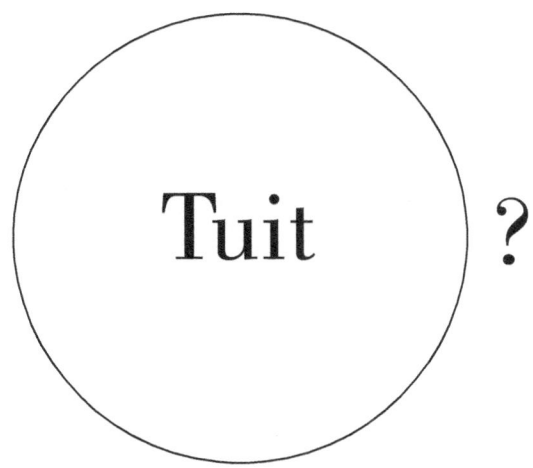

Tuit ?

The Little Beige Book

Business as Learned Via a Lifetime Journey (Upward)
Through the Bowels of a Fortune 500 Corporation

Thomas H. Haag

Library of Congress Control Number:		2010914841
ISBN:	Hardcover	978-1-4535-9161-1
	Softcover	978-1-4535-9160-4
	Ebook	978-1-4535-9162-8

This book was printed in the United States of America.

To order additional copies of this book, contact:
Xlibris Corporation
1-888-795-4274
www.Xlibris.com
Orders@Xlibris.com
80496

Contents

Introduction 11
About The Cover 13

Chapter 1: On Business 15
1. Of Youth And Age.. 15
2. The Big Secret Of Business 17
3. Anatomy Of Failure 19
4. Rules For Business 20

Chapter 2: Lead Like A Leader.. 22
1. Delegate, Delegate, Delegate 22
2. Information And Communication Overload........................... 24
3. Some Thoughts About Firing Someone 25
4. Public Speaking/Presentations 26
5. Feasting On Competitors' Mistakes................................ 28
6. Negotiation 30
7. Morale 31
8. Management By Objectives—Mbo..................................... 33
9. Reorganizations 35

Chapter 3: Your Cast Of Characters 36
1. Psychology Of Sales Staff.. 36
2. Researchers And The Research Spectrum............................ 38
3. Entrepreneurs.. 41
4. Psychology Of Non-Exempts.. 42
5. Thinkers & Non-Thinkers.. 43
6. A Non-Pc Look At Rejection 46
7. Getting Value From Outside Directors—A Mini-Case Study 48

Chapter 4: Nuts And Bolts 50
1 (a).   Finance: On Finance 50
1(b).   Finance: Measures Of Profitability—Key Ratios 52
1(c).   Finance: Some More Financials.. 56
2(a).   Pricing: Pricing Theory And Practice 57
2(b).   Pricing: Pricing Tactics... 58
2(c).   Pricing: The Art Of Price Increases 60
2(d).   Pricing: Copper Prices.. 61
3(a).   Producivity: Mis And Computers 62
3(b).   Producivity: Product Line Rationalization 64
3(c).   Producivity: Product Line Churn 65

Chapter 5: Where Do You Go From Here? 66
1.   Acquisitions.. 66
2.   Joint Ventures/Partnerships/Mergers 69
3.   Future Risks 72
4.   On Weathering A Recession 73
5.   Epilogue: Final Haagram (Written During A Recession).............. 74

Post-Script 77
Endnotes 79

Dedication

To my wife and daughters for their support. Also, to my former bosses, from whom I learned what and what not to do as I worked my way up from the bowels (and I do mean bowels) of a Fortune 500 Company.

"You can observe a lot
just by watching."[1]

Yogi Berra

My first truly responsible job at age nineteen—making sure that eighteen 105 mm howitzer shells landed in the right spot.

Introduction

My academic credentials in business are scant, but I did end up running the biggest and most profitable division of a Fortune 500 company, Rohm & Haas Company ("R&H"), with 200 researchers, 45 field representatives across the U.S. and Canada, 5 production plants, 750 products, and 12,000 customers. At that time my team accounted for 1/8 of the world-wide corporate sales, but produced one-quarter of the profits. The margins for the chemical specialties were 16% OPAT and 32% RONA, and the great physical bulk of the products (approx. 90%) sold were composed of commodity chemicals, with marketing-defined and research-developed bells and whistles attached. I studied every boss I ever had, keeping their wheat and discarding their chaff.

I also started up two financially-successful specialty joint ventures with Japanese partners, and served as an outside director for a mid-sized specialty manufacturing firm for six years. In this latter role, I felt compelled to proffer aid to a bright, new, young CEO for the corporation who had been thrust into the position by the untimely death of his older brother.

As a self-appointed mentor, the format I employed was to write "HAAGRAMS" on various business topics as they appeared. The understanding was that he could freely use or "circular file" them. I never had a contract, and we agreed that if either party was unhappy, we would say so, shake hands, and say goodbye. He tolerated me for six years until I retired at the end of my term. Many of the essays in this tome began as Haagrams, which I have tweaked for your reading pleasure.

About The Cover

I worked with many MBA's from top business schools and they varied from excellent to mediocre. I am very fond of an article in the Harvard Business Review by Professor J. Sterling Livingstone titled "Myth of the Well Educated Manager."[2] His main tenet was that case studies did not really prepare managers for the real world because they clearly identified a problem that had to be solved. In practice, the problem is to figure out *what the problem is*, or even better, *what the problem is going to become*, in time to avoid or mitigate it. I had never encountered "stagflation" or "oil embargoes" or "terrorist attacks" or the collapse of major financial entities, during my academic life.

It is noteworthy that many concepts of business were developed by the military, not business schools: the division of line and staff, computers, PERT, logistics, the Internet. Think of General Marshall, who had 16 million employees involved in a world-wide enterprise, while the ENIAC was still under development at the University of Pennsylvania.

I am proud that three people whom I had personally recruited into my business team later left to accept VP jobs at Fortune 500 companies. What I found to be the most important feature of successful managers is that they had all gotten "around to it". Everyone has good intentions and has numerous things they are going to do when they *get around to it*. A fellow manager at my firm had yellow discs inscribed "Tuit." He gave them to his subordinates and customers when he felt the need to move things along, stating that "Now that you've gotten a round tuit, let's get moving!"

Chapter 1

On Business

1. OF YOUTH AND AGE

I have read a fair amount on business, but some thoughts on the finest paper follows:

In the 17th century, Sir Francis Bacon wrote a pithy essay on business titled, "Of Youth and Age", in which he made a very cogent case for blending these elements to achieve success in business. While it probably would have been acceptable to him to consider substituting "fresh view" for youth, and "experience" for age (even while accepting Wilde's definition of experience as 'the name that men give to their mistakes'), it would be presumptuous to do so for him. A selection of quotes from the Bacon essay follows. Presumably, the copyright has expired.[3]

"The errors of young men are the ruin of business; but the errors of aged men amount but to this, that more might have been done, or sooner.[1] Young men, in the conduct and manage of actions, embrace more than they can hold; stir more than they can quiet; fly to the end, without consideration of the means and degrees; pursue some few principles which they have chanced upon absurdly; use extreme remedies at first; and *that which doubleth all errors will not acknowledge or retract them*; like an unready horse, that will neither stop nor turn. Men of age object too much, consult too long, adventure too little, repent too soon, and seldom drive business home to the full period,

---

[1]   Recall that a single young bond trader in Singapore brought down the venerable Barings Bank, which was known for being the bank of the Royals.

but content themselves with a mediocrity of success. *Certainly it is good to compound employments of both*; for that will be good for the present, because the virtues of either age may correct the defects of both; and good for succession, that young men may be learners, while men in age are actors; and lastly, good for extern accidents, because authority followeth old men, and favor and popularity youth. But for the moral part, perhaps youth will have the pre-eminence, as age hath for the politic."

It is likely that this essay is not part of the curriculum at business schools, nor is it likely that Jimmy Ling . . . the guru of business diversification purely for the sake of diversity and size, i.e., conglomerates, is discussed either, although he was once the darling of Wall Street. Conglomerate can be a business-school synonym for "hodge-podge". Synergy is a much used word for something that is difficult to find and to implement.

2. THE BIG SECRET OF BUSINESS

The Big Secret of Business is that there is no secret to running a successful long term growing enterprise. Most growth can be obtained via the ever-present pressure toward industry consolidation to achieve economies of scale, and by feasting rapidly on the mistakes of competitors. Of course, you can also grow via internal innovation, but absent a flash of creation (transistor, antibiotics, light bulb, etc.) it is a slow, incremental path.

Manufacturers are all oriented around tangible products, and all have common parts such as:

- *Marketing*: defining product needs, securing them, placing, pricing, promoting. For this analysis I'll put selling, and fending off competitors and feasting on their mistakes here.
- *Research*: innovating, new products, customer service, assessing competitive threats.
- *Finance*: keeping accurate scorecards on costs and profitability, securing favorable financing as required to support corporate objectives, minimizing taxes.
- *Administration*: securing and keeping good personnel, getting products to customers and collecting, purchasing, legal, support staff, training.
- *Production*: producing products efficiently, with low costs and suitable quality.
- *Management*: providing vision and direction to the enterprise, insuring that all functions are properly sized and staffed to mesh efficiently, remembering *always* that the only reason that the corporation exists is to return value on a continuing basis to the owners/shareholders.

All corporations must perform these functions more or less well or they won't be around long. Now let's look at three firms and rate them.

OPTIMA CORP.

This company really has its act together, and does everything above average (avg. = 1.0) so we multiply them out . . . 1.1 x 1.1 x 1.1 x 1.1 x 1.1 x 1.1 = 1.77

SO-SO CORP.

This concern does everything satisfactorily; they feel that they are "pretty good" and are self-satisfied. Their score is . . . 1.0 x 1.0 x 1.0 x 1.0 x 1.0 x 1.0. = 1.0

SCHLOCK CO.

They do everything a little below average. Their 0.9 performance multiplies out to a score of 0.5. So, of course, they have to price low. People at SO-SO look down upon them, but when SCHLOCK goes belly up, they find that OPTIMA has the profits to outbid them and upgrade the remains of SCHLOCK and gain market share. In fact, OPTIMA has done this several times and SO-SO is surprised that they are now regarded as a Schlock Company at the bottom of the industry, and they have to start cutting their prices.

There is a moral here somewhere, but I forget what it is.

Running a business is like trying to go up the down escalator. If you stand still, you end up on your ass on the floor below. If you jog, you stay in place. To get to the next level, you have to run!

3. ANATOMY OF FAILURE

A pet supplies firm decided to make a major thrust to gain market share at high profit in a new dog chow line. They did it right. They signed up with the best veterinarian university, the nutritionists designed the perfect scientifically-balanced ingredients, the marketing department planned a launch blitz with TV and magazine advertising, the production department came up with a sterile fast production line, using the attractive new package designed by sales, who also laid out a coupon campaign and secured highly desired shelf space in the largest market stores. The product took off like a rocket! But, unfortunately, it followed a parabolic path back to earth.

This led to a recrimination-filled management meeting with every discipline pointing a finger at some other department. After much useless wrangling, one fellow raised his hand and said, "The dogs don't like it."

I once sat (restively) through a presentation with colorful slides and multi-media, which featured films of helicopters landing at the "Inn on the Park" in New York City, to launch an elastic fiber named "Animate" to compete with DuPont's "Lycra." Models in colorful gowns swirled through. Earlier I asked the research lab head on the project how they could possibly use a high level of vinylidene chloride as the base polymer when it was known for its intrinsic tendency to discolor upon aging. He smiled as if I were stupid. Later, during a test market with a major lingerie manufacturer, I had my wife buy articles made with "Animate." They discolored badly after a few months in a drawer.

The speaker at this internal presentation closed with three lines that I labeled as "Strike One," "Strike Two," and "Strike Three." He pronounced that: 1. Our fiber will be the highest-priced fiber; it's a Cadillac; 2. It's different; we will have to educate our customers on how to use it (I never sought to "educate" our customers. Rather, I "informed" them.); and 3. Customers will have to buy new equipment to process it. What arrogance!

The reason I left research to go to marketing and business was that I had worked on too many projects which were technical successes and commercial failures. The marketing personnel knew a great deal about marketing in "general" but did not understand the marketing required in a "particular" specialty business.

The devil is truly in the details. The failure is in general.

4. RULES FOR BUSINESS

1. The Golden Rule . . ."He who has the gold rules."
2. Your customers have the gold that you seek.
3. Your customers are not charitable; they insist on real value for their gold.
4. You must demonstrate that your offering will help them get more gold.
5. They do not like to be surprised by price increases which will upset their business plans.
6. Customers are not required to be lovable, but if they pay your bills, they must be loved.
7. Do not learn the "tricks" of the trade; learn the trade.
8. Sell what you got. Don't sell what you don't got. Talk about the new and improved product when you got it.
9. Never ever lie to a customer. A favorable 20-year reputation in an industry will disappear in a flash.
10. Never tolerate abusive treatment or language from a customer for yourself or your representatives—quietly close your briefcase, say "good day" and leave.
11. No job that requires you to be unethical or immoral, be a toady, or risk prison, is worth having.
12. Maintain the rules and standards of your corporation, but if they ever come into conflict with your personal ethical positions, you must maintain your own standards.
13. Never make gratuitous "clever remarks" about a problem or a person in public.
14. When travelling on business, and you pass a restroom, use it. You never know how long it will be before another one is available. Also, only take one or two sips when coffee is offered at a meeting, especially if you expect it to last more than an hour. Let the other participants get antsy and more amenable to your position. On the flipside, if you chair what you know will be a long, fractious meeting, graciously serve everybody a large steaming hot cup of coffee before the meetings starts. Then run to the nearest bathroom and empty your own bladder. Allow about an hour of political posturing and "c.y.a." discussion and then you will find people more agreeable to compromises and problem-solving
15. Do your homework thoroughly in advance of proposing a course of action. The conduct of corporate business is no place for "swag"—scientific wild ass guesses. The equation is one "oh shit" equals ten "attaboys."
16. No snivelling allowed.

Violations of these basic rules can lead to embarrassment, financial loss or full-scale disaster. A good negative example of not doing all your homework fell into my lap one day as I strolled by a conference room. Out popped the VP for North America with a couple of others involved in an animated discussion. He spotted me and asked me to come into the meeting, as he had a topic he wanted to discuss with me afterwards. A few minutes into the meeting I realized that they were deeply concerned about the safety of shipping potentially-explosive ethylene oxide through the streets and railways of Philadelphia to get to the Bridesburg plant. They were proposing the costly construction of armored rail cars, when I opined that they not ship any of the highly-flammable chemical through the city, but instead load the trucks or rail cars onto barges at the Marcus Hook oil refinery south of the city, and unload at the idle pier at the Bridesburg plant. Any unlikely explosion would take place in the Delaware River, a half mile from the Pennsylvania and New Jersey riverbanks. This suggestion was followed by a long period of silence.[2]

---

[2]   For an impressive example of the explosive power of ethylene oxide, watch the CSB Safety Video: Ethylene Oxide Explosion, regarding the March 5, 2007 explosion at the Sterigenics plant in Ontario, California. Viewed on June 21, 2010 at: www.youtube.com/watch?v=2UnKLm2Eag.

Chapter 2

Lead Like a Leader

1. DELEGATE, DELEGATE, DELEGATE

The most difficult thing to learn as a chief executive is: "DO NOT DO ANYTHING YOURSELF THAT YOU DO NOT HAVE TO DO PERSONALLY." Never look up an airline flight or book a hotel for yourself! Your administrative assistant should know how you like to travel, and arrange all the details for you—providing information to you on earlier and later flights as a back-up.

Never let subordinates come into your office, tell you about a problem or a decision that has to be made, scatter a bushel basket of data on your desk, and sit there waiting for you to tell them what to do. Tell them to take their data and get out—and to return only when they have organized the info, analyzed it, are able to tell you what conclusions they have reached, and what recommendations they have. Then, and only then, can you have a *meaningful dialogue* with them.

While you can delegate authority, you are still responsible for results. Expect mistakes to be followed by improvement. If subordinates don't improve, get rid of them—and be assured that the great majority of them will appreciate the opportunity to learn from mistakes and will become happier, more valuable persons, who will then feel loyal to you. But do not tolerate those who can't cut it. Resist the temptation to try to work around them—do each of you a favor and axe them.

GET YOUR STAFF RIGHT, and use your time for greater things. Strategic planning, as opposed to fighting fires; building customer and industry contacts, versus signing credits; getting to know the financial community, government officials, fellow local businesspersons, etc., rather than being mired in the details.

Finally, have a "Wall Street Journal" delivered to your desk each morning, and scan the two left-side vertical columns, which give brief summaries of the financial and general news of the day. You can turn to the details for any item that piques your interest. This is an excellent and simple way to stay informed on important issues in the world of business and politics, and to spend your time profitably while answering nature's call.[3]

---

[3]   Ok, I'm aware that many of you will access the WSJ on-line. But I submit for your consideration, it can't be that convenient to drag your laptop with you, and where's the satisfaction in staring at your little phone screen in the restroom stall? Also, if the toilet paper dispenser is empty, you possess an emergency supply. Just remember to crinkle it thoroughly.

2. INFORMATION AND COMMUNICATION OVERLOAD

The first symptoms of the modern business disease of information and communication overload are sometimes propagated under the theme that everyone in the corporation has to be instantly and completely informed of all happenings, so that they have a sense of "belonging" on the team. The use of the telephone, voicemail, e-mail, copy machines, computer calendaring, etc., proliferates this trend and gives everyone instant access into your office, your eyes, your ears, your brain's thinking and, importantly, your brain's resting time. This problem is greatly compounded by being a nice, sympathetic, polite, inclusive person.

If you feel that this is, or is becoming, a real problem for you, here are some suggestions that helped me deal with a myriad of contacts.

DELEGATE, DELEGATE, DELEGATE, blocks of work which do not have to be reported to you until they are complete or stymied, or until you ask for them. A good illustration is to compare the administrations of two military officers: Eisenhower, who was used to commanding millions of troops, and Carter, who had commanded an atomic sub. Jimmy sank out of sight trying to know everything, as I'm sure he did with his sub.

Limit access to yourself, in a controlled way. Walk-around-management is a great thing, walking into the boss's office at any time is not. Only attend meetings where your presence is necessary. I refused to calendar myself as my problem was too much time in meetings and not enough time in the field. I didn't want people scheduling me for meetings I did not need to attend. My boss, my secretary, and my wife were the only people who *needed* to know exactly where I was and why, and I provided them with my weekly itinerary. When I actually had to think, rather than react, I hung a sign on my office door saying, "Do Not Disturb Me . . . unless you can fire me, or want to invite me for a coffee break." Interestingly, it even kept some away who could fire me. In extreme cases, I worked at home, saving two hours of commuting time and being entirely free from interruptions (that included my wife and kids), and eating a sandwich for lunch while working, and only being called out to kiss the kiddies goodnight.

At one time I considered starting a committee to investigate how we could cut down on meetings; however, I realized that we would have to meet once a month to measure our progress. We all object to "spam" in our e-mail, but there is a hell of a lot of "spam" of other types in our daily work routines. You don't have to eat it.

3. SOME THOUGHTS ABOUT FIRING SOMEONE

Firing an employee is the worst part of the job, and if it ever gets easy, then you had better worry about yourself. It is also necessary, and therefore does not violate a time-honored scruple: "To inflict pain without purpose is immoral."

It can be handled humanely by meeting in private and suggesting that the employee has a few weeks to seek other employment on the basis that it is easier to secure a job while you have one. Interestingly, I found that most had determined themselves that they were not making the grade, and that placed them under great stress. One employee actually thanked me for firing him!

I always felt a sense of personal failure when I had to fire someone, as if I should have been able to help the person develop and grow. After awhile I finally noted, however, that if employees were dumb—I could not make them smart; if employees were lazy—I could not make them ambitious; if employees were incompetent in their specialties—I could not supply what had eluded them at law, business, accounting, or technical school; if employees had managed to avoid learning how to write a decent paragraph in their native tongue after 16 years or more of formal education—I could not teach them either; if employees had a bad attitude—I could not play amateur psychiatrist to find out why they hated their mothers.

This all boils down to an old cliché—"You can lead a horse to water, but you can't make him drink." However, you are free to feel like choking the fool!

4. PUBLIC SPEAKING/PRESENTATIONS

The basic problem with public speaking is that your body reads staring as a hostile act. When you stand up to speak . . . everyone stares at you. Your body prepares you to fight or flee. You become pale because the release of adrenaline is making blood leave your skin to reduce bleeding when you are wounded; it is also speeding up your heart and respiration rates, so that you can run away faster or fight more vigorously. If you don't believe that staring is a naturally hostile act, stare at a dog. He will either put his tail down and slink away, or raise his hackles and begin to growl at you (start with small dogs, not rottweilers). Then what can you do? Starting with a small self-deprecating joke or comment can help. If you know some people in the audience, focus on them—you will appear to have general eye contact with the audience but actually you are chatting with a few old friends. If your audience is composed of strangers, focus your gaze just above their heads so it appears to be eye contact, but you will not actually see their eyes staring at you. Use slides or visual aids that draw the audience's gaze away from you, and serve as prompters for you.

Your most important consideration is to consider your audience, who they are, why they are there, what they expect to hear, and *then* consider what *you* want them to hear.

WHO? WHAT? WHERE? HOW? WHEN? WHY? SO WHAT? Make sure all these questions are answered clearly and succinctly and you will have spoken (or written) effectively. All but the last question is old-fashioned newspaper reporting; the last one is critical in business. "So what" does this topic mean to the corporation or the audience?

Of course a number of these can be rolled into a few sentences, but never omit one: you must introduce yourself and the purpose for your address. For example, "I'm the CEO of the XYZ Corporation, and I'm here tonight to tell you what we do, and about a cooperative program we started about six months ago in concert with our mutual township officials to ensure that we are an asset to your community and a good neighbor."

REPEAT, REPEAT, REPEAT. Never assume that people will follow you through to a logical conclusion, and retain what you said. Say what you want up front, give the data to support it, say that the data support it, and then conclude by saying it again! I'm here to review the first quarter results which were really quite good . . . now that I've shown you the data, as you can see it was an excellent quarter . . . . In closing, I should like to note that our programs appear to be working well and have produced very good results in the first quarter.

You are going to hear and give so many presentations that you will develop a strong negative reaction to poor, vague, wandering, inconclusive ones . . . and your staff should respond to your needs and improve to help you.

One last item . . . practice, practice, practice. Reading books won't help you speak better, but the more you are on your feet in front of an audience, the better you'll get. Know your subject well, but do not memorize. Use bullet-point slides as prompters, but do not put a lot of prose on a slide and then read it to the audience. Very few people are eloquent speakers, but by following these guidelines you can *be effective*, *be brief*, and *be seated*.

5. FEASTING ON COMPETITORS' MISTAKES

One of our competitors, Union Carbide, got so frustrated at their inability to get their lower priced products accepted by the research departments of our major customers, that they made a series of presentations to the top executives of these firms (deliberately staging them so the heads of research and purchasing would not be present), where they demonstrated the large savings to the customers that could be had by simply substituting their products for ours. There was an implication that their research and purchasing people were not responsive because of laziness or worse. Of course the people who headed these areas had been selected by the very people whom they were addressing! Many were held in high regard by them. Of course the purchasing and research people learned of these approaches from within their own firms, or from us rapidly spreading the story through the industry along with the rejoinder, "They are intelligent people who know what their products are worth, and that's why they are low priced." They forgot Ben Franklin's axiom that, "Three people can keep a secret provided that two of them are dead."

No doubt their salespeople were warmly received on their future sales calls.

Another major firm, DuPont, had an extensive dealer network and a well recognized brand name, but decided that it would buy its way into mass marketers by discounting steeply. Of course their dealers learned of this. Their competitors immediately started raiding their old dealers, and they quickly learned about the purchasing leverage of mass marketers. They ruined their business and sold out for pennies on the dollar.

The competitors I know who tried and failed to take my area away from R&H included DuPont, Dow, Union Carbide, Air Products, Monsanto, BASF, Imperial Chemicals, Reichold, Borden, National Starch, and others. We won lawsuits against domestic and foreign firms who tried to steal trade secrets.

We also won back three large customers who tried to go with captive manufacture. Our best tactic was to maintain cordial relations, but not to sample any new technology-based products until we announced them publicly. The new products outperformed the old products they were struggling to match, and their competitors had a one-year lead on them because we had worked cooperatively with their researchers on the developmental materials.

We prevailed in these contests because of a symbiotic internal relationship between R&H research and marketing, and a host of top-flight people who worked hard on the basics.

Dow recently satisfied its lust by buying the entire R&H corporation for $19 billion. This happened after a series of CEO's with MBA's in Finance and "overseas experience" had "managed" the firm from one of the best chemical specialty firms in the world down to a "D" stock rating. Much of this could be attributed to the fact that overseas they were effectively given a deck of cards representing proven products, manufacturing processes, successful marketing programs, and well-calculated prices vis-à-vis competitive materials, and asked to play them. But back home the questions were: Do we want to play in this game? If so, what cards do we need to win? How can we get those cards? A much tougher and time-consuming struggle, which "fast-trackers" couldn't deal with. Their knowledge of the corporation was *broad*, as the independent foreign firms covered the range of operations, but they were also too *shallow* to compete in specialty products. They heard the words that customers said, but did not understand what they meant. Most of them could not find the research center without a GPS, and considered the people there "a little odd." That is, however, where new products came from. The third time an aggressive European R&H executive exclaimed that he never got anything from research, I asked him to tell me about his licensing program. When he said that he didn't have one, I replied that I was puzzled, because he had a wide portfolio of products to sell. Where did they come from?

If you hire well-educated, ambitious, aggressive people who want to become very rich in a short period of time, you might end up with a number of corporate opportunistic, political game players who do not worry about cutting corners, bending legalities and trying to plagiarize other people's ideas. You too, might wind up as the main course on your competitor's banquet table.

6. NEGOTIATION

There are many volumes and courses on this topic, but a few basic principles will guide you. Do not have *a* plan before entering discussions, have three. Plan A is the best possible outcome, Plan B is a good outcome, and Plan C is the least that you will accept before breaking off negotiations—which sometimes will result in a callback with some additional sweeteners. Put a couple of throw-aways in your initial statement, which you can graciously yield on later.

There are a couple of physical moves which might trigger additional dialogue. One is the mere act of straitening your papers and placing them in your briefcase, with a pause before closing it. The final act is placing your hands on your knees as part of the process of standing up. This last move has been ingrained by TV, as it was the signal to move the overhead sound boom so the person about to stand would not hit his head on the microphone.

One tactic I found to be very useful when dealing with Japanese firms was to employ their need for consensus against them. I never made a decision while in Japan and I never said "no" to any of their proposals. I learned to say "That is very interesting. I will have to think about that." Because they could not go forward until they had a complete consensus, they would sweeten the deal a little more.

No matter how superior your position, never take all the chips off the table, or back your adversary into a corner. Give him a couple of minor exceptions as a trap door to save face and self-esteem. Otherwise, you have generated a vengeful lifetime enemy, who might show up in the wrong place at the right time to pay you back.

7. MORALE

Sagging morale can sometimes settle in like a damp fog. What can you do to lift it? My number one suggestion by far is to . . . DELEGATE, DELEGATE, DELEGATE. You might have heard me say this before[4], but nothing does more for employee job enrichment, than what cascades down from you, and in reaction forces your managers to do the same, and their reports to do so, to the point where you have happy janitors, who are empowered to decide what are the best brooms and disinfectants to use, and to plan their own clean-up itineraries. This delegation has to be made along with the authority to control the job. The biggest frustration which kills morale is to have responsibility for a task without the authority to control it.

Now you are human and will be concerned, so I suggest you consider what I did as an "S3" supervisor. You explain the task, sketch out a couple of possible routes and problems, express confidence in the person, tell them it is their baby, and walk away. Then you sneakily make "casual" inquiries of the progress from time to time via indirect probes such as, "Hey Jill, how are things going?"

Give a brief "state of the company" talk once a year. Schedule an hour and a half on a Friday afternoon at the end of the day. Give all employees 15 minutes or so for coffee and goodies. Then give about a half-hour positive assessment of the company, as contrasted with your particular industry, and with the macro-economy. Make sure to give shout-outs, such as "Hey Production . . . way to go, scrap is down, ISO 9,000,000 certification! Wow, Research, look at this sales chart for new products! Kudos, Administration, on-time deliveries are up, returns down, collections faster! Impressive, Sales did a great job while a number of competitors went out of business, but our margins went up, and we wiped out the loss of our major customer via new sales!"

A great time to do this is at the close of the fiscal year. Even (especially) during tough economic times, point out, for example, that industrial employment has declined for 16 months, a list of competitors has closed their doors, and yet there are no lay-offs at your firm. You continue to buy equipment and research for the future. When industrial production turns up, you should be well positioned. Field questions for about 15 minutes, and then let them leave for home a half-hour early to start the weekend. You might want to videotape it so it can be sent to branches, sales meetings, night shifts, etc.

---

[4]   Indeed, see Chap. 2, Essay #1 above.

You can also get a great boost in morale and interdisciplinary cooperation simply by consolidating the managers for production, research, and administration in the same building. Physical proximity really cuts down on the "us" versus "them" crap.

8. MANAGEMENT BY OBJECTIVES—MBO

Management by Objectives, or MBO, is one of the business fads that I had to suffer through. No doubt my firm screwed up its implementation, as I concluded when I was once supposed to negotiate objectives with an artist! However, like all programs, you can learn from it. The first thing I learned was that I could not give blanket approval to Professor Peter Drucker, who was the fashionable academic guru of the day and the creator of the MBO movement. I labored through one of his tomes on management right up to the point where he expounded that the modern corporation exists to fill a social function.[4] There I closed the book, never to open it again, though I'm sure my judgment would not have troubled this famous man. MBO provided me with a memorable laugh, however, when at one of our sales conferences our H.B.S. chairman made a speech lauding the program, which by then was held in contempt by line management. During the question and answer period, a much-admired old line manager (who was about to retire), stood up and announced that he had researched Drucker's MBO program intensively, and surprisingly discovered that the idea had actually been created by his mother! And that is why it had come to be called, "The Mother Drucker MBO Program."

But, I also found one idea which worked well for me and my business team (district sales managers, field force managers, marketing managers, production managers, research managers, finance, advertising and promotion managers, etc.) It was *personal* KRA's . . . Key Results Areas. What each manager could do (including . . . or better, especially me), after pledging their "lives and sacred honor" to making the Business Plan, was to actually stop and think for awhile about what they were doing. Then pick three, four, five or so things which *they personally* could control and accomplish to aid the business or to improve themselves. We would pull these out and review our progress on these items as a group, informally, after each intensive quarterly business plan review. Boy, did that put the heat on me to show progress, as I had to lead off.

My KRA's might look like the following:

1. Strengthen my personal relationships with key people at a key account.
2. Give personal thanks promptly to each person in the business who made a real contribution by a notable achievement (my managers were quick to point out any of my sins, so I could correct them).
3. Complete the American Management Association finance course.

4. Thieve a good plant area manager to replace one of mine who was going to retire during the year.

Of course, I can think of a number of items for you to put on your list of personal KRA's. Work fascinates me; I could watch it all day long. But the only real value will come from inside your own head.

9. REORGANIZATIONS

Beware of academics trying to sell their latest programs. I suffered through a number of fads, the worst of which was the "Dual Matrix" management structure, wherein at high levels everyone had two bosses: a vertical one as part of a business team, and a horizontal one defined by role. For example, a marketing manager would report both to the VP of his or her business team (vertical) and supposedly, to another manager (horizontal). [You can surmise how valuable a marketing tip from me would be to a manager in Singapore]. Now imagine this matrix imposed upon four world zones (North America, Latin America, Europe and Asia), and you can determine that the organizational chart looked like the wiring diagram for a pinball machine or Hilary Clinton's proposed health care plan, which might have gotten her thrown out of a Business 101 course. But, I remember getting a call from my daughter telling me that her professor of Multinational Management at the Wharton School had placed my company's dual matrix chart on an overhead to demonstrate a sophisticated multinational management structure.

It probably made sense to have a VP for each of the four geographic regions, and a VP for each line of business (i.e. coatings, plastics, agricultural products, etc.), but when the matrix was pushed down to lower levels of the organization, it broke down. In the real world, the dual matrix system ignored the Golden Rule of Business: he who has the gold rules. The person who wrote your performance review, which in turn determined your raise and continuation of employment, always won out. In the end, most of the dual matrix was allowed to evaporate away, particularly at lower operating levels.

As you might expect if you have read this far, this episode brings to mind another analogy. A reorganization is like fornication between elephants. There is a great deal of trumpeting, all of the action takes place at high levels, small beings get trampled underfoot, and 22 months later, all you get is another elephant.

Chapter 3

Your Cast of Characters

1. PSYCHOLOGY OF SALES STAFF

Salespersons can have an "us versus them" mentality, with "us" being the heroic lone eagles out on the firing line getting no help from "them"—and "them" being the soft-living, dumb, fat cats at the home office.

I was told at my first national sales conference that never having been a field rep, I couldn't possibly appreciate or understand them. I responded that I had never been a woman either, but I definitely appreciated them, and even though I didn't fully understand them, I hoped to do better with the reps.[5]

I found that, in general, the sales staff were conflicted persons . . . they wanted to be independent, but then feared that no one cared about them. To a great extent, they sought recognition and approval. We all do, but they almost had a pathological need for it. So, buy them a meal and chat with them, make a phone call to say thanks for a new account, and send a handwritten note to congratulate them for closing a contract. Award them hokey prizes in front of their peers.

I ran the following year's national sales conference and focused on the needs of the sales force rather than the needs of the home office. I offer some tips to keep your sales staff content:

1. Charge their batteries—by emphasizing positive results rather than dwelling on problems.

---

[5] This joke worked well in the early 1970's. Caution: don't try it today.

2. Make the home office executives freely available to them, one on one, on an informal basis, i.e., after formal meetings play golf with them, join the poker game at night, share a drink with them in the bar. This is the only way you will hear their real concerns, *as most are too shy to vent in a crowd*!
3. Give them plenty of time to mingle and interact with their peers.
4. Pass out some awards, I-pods, jewelry, golf balls, gag gifts, send them all home with $100 gift certificates to thank them (and provide them with proof for their spouses and families about just how good they are).
5. Give them a "Representative at Court". This is someone to whom they can tell their troubles, who will give them a sympathetic ear and relay concerns to "Management", help them with training, etc. A field force manager is a good candidate for this role.

I'm not sure if these actions really pushed our sales up, but they did promote harmony, and certainly helped in selling price increases to the reps, who are your toughest customers.

As for a typical "sales personality"—I don't think there is such a thing. I found that the top salespersons were everything from hell-raising party animals to quiet religious family types. The common denominator was that they tried hard to help their customers, with all types of problems (which of course required that they actually understood the customer's business). *Helping* customers means more than just *selling* them.

2. RESEARCHERS AND THE RESEARCH SPECTRUM

You might have noticed that researchers are "different" from others in the business world. The great challenge to a researcher is to be an objective optimist—optimistic enough to make the fifth attempt at solving a problem, but objective enough to say "No, that did not work either" and then march on to number six.

Decades ago I attended an in-house lecture where the speaker, a Dr. Iwanciow, categorized researchers based on their focus on five areas. His graphic representations said it perfectly. Here's my rendition of them:

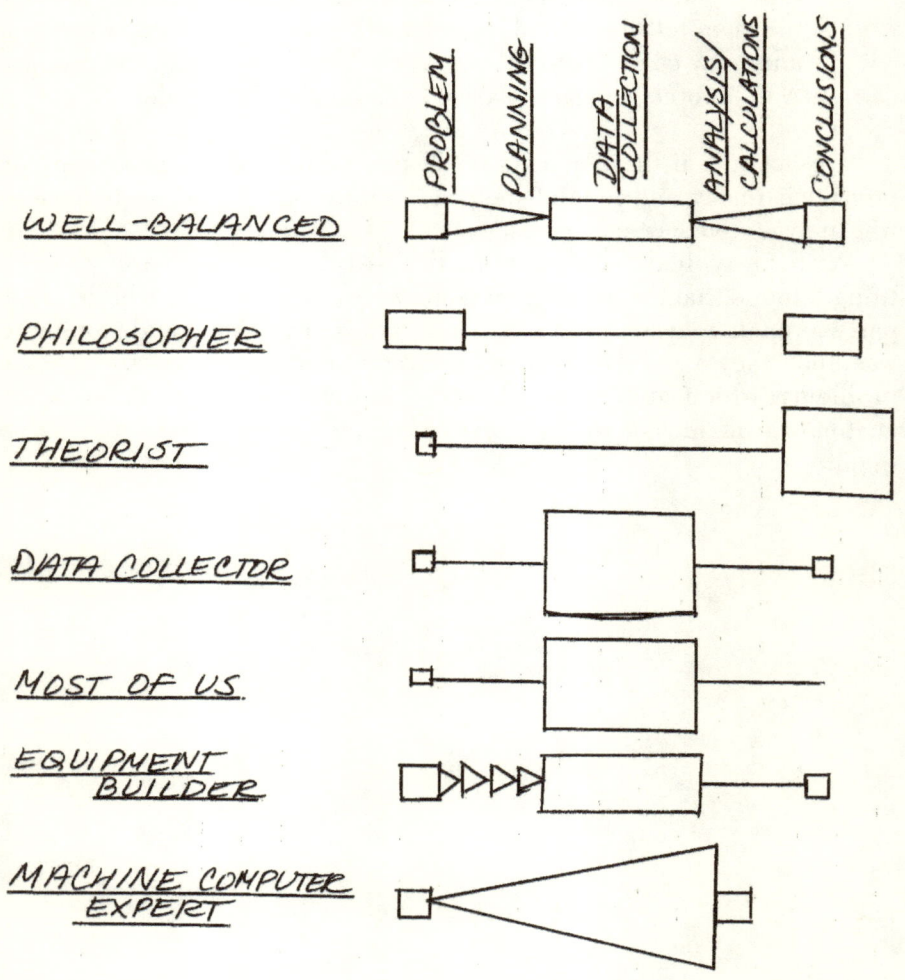

You will note that the non-existent average researcher is different from the average non-existent employee. They march, or stumble, to a different drummer. They need a "manager" with a softer hand and some technical smarts to help lead them (not herd them) to the promised land. About one in five will be worth a great deal to your firm.

Now that you recognize the types of folks in your research department, what should you do with them? I have created the research spectrum to demonstrate the various functions of research in a company:

THE RESEARCH SPECTRUM

Plant and Process Support ↓	Sales/ Service ↓	Technical Service ↓	Product Development ↓	Exploratory ↓	Scouting ↓	Basic Research ↓
Necessary to keep plant or product running smoothly	Aid Given to a particular customer for a particular problem blocking a sale	Seeking solution to a general problem to allow expanded sales of an existing product or technology E.g., Raise 20° gloss of this film by 10 units and sell into a new market segment; Learn how to adhere this film to poly-carbonate	When market needs cannot be met by existing products— but likely can be met by recombining existing technologies	When you need some new approach or solution to a basic problem— before you can begin product development. E.g., We need 90% retro-reflectivity.	Give research 4 hours per week to try their own wild ideas	E.g., What causes exterior degradation of organic matter?

Research expenses for chemical companies typically run about 3-6% of sales. Commodity companies are on the low end, specialty companies are on the high end, agricultural chemical companies are higher still, and drug companies are even higher than that. I would guess that 4% would be about right for a typical manufacturing concern with a mix of commodity and specialty items, until and unless marketing comes up with a number of good projects to warrant pushing it up to 5% or so. You need to spend about 1-2% just on plant support. You can't just turn a product or process over to manufacturing and walk away. Materials drift, process changes are made, etc.

A good morale booster is to allow researchers four hours per week to play with their personal ideas. In practice, you will find that only about 1 in 3 or 4 actually have the imagination to use it. If it results in a good lead, of course it can evolve into a product development or exploratory project.

Be careful with Purchasing-developed projects. For example, Purchasing finds a cheaper source for a raw material. They immediately calculate the annual savings, but sometimes the cost to check out the new material or correct its flaws obviates the advantage. There is also a lost opportunity cost in that you have your researchers facing backwards.

Remember, there are six phases to most major research projects:

1. Enthusiasm
2. Disillusionment
3. Panic
4. Search for the guilty
5. Punishment of the innocent
6. Praise and honors for the nonparticipants

3. ENTREPRENEURS

Entrepreneurs are truly different from others. Their only real passion is the single-minded continuous drive to establish their companies. They lie to themselves and to their families by saying they are working so hard for the welfare and security of their families. In truth they sacrifice them to pursue their own objectives. They are **pyramid builders.** Their companies are the monuments which attest to their own lives. If you have the ability to bring a few stones to them, they will be effusive in their affection, for as long as you are doing so. If you can't help them add to the structure, they will ignore you to death.

At some point, perhaps when entrepreneurs have grown as large and rich (and large far outweighs rich) as is feasible, or the fires are banking with age, they are prone to become pillars of the community. Perhaps they'll establish charity foundations. Perhaps they'll have a school at a university or a hospital wing named for them to prolong their supposed immortality and importance.

"Ashes to ashes, dust to dust." "I'll never forget good old what's his name." "Sic Transit Gloria."

4. PSYCHOLOGY OF NON-EXEMPTS

This is a presumptuous and pompous sounding topic, but that never stops me, and you remember that, as Mark Twain noted, "No generality is worth a damn, including this one."

In general, I found that I had to treat non-exempts in a different fashion from professionals. I found that I got no points for what I considered major items, but got many demerits for what I considered to be trivial items, to wit:

Here is a nice raise. So what, I work hard, I deserve it.

I'm polite and considerate. So what, that's the way you are supposed to be.

I'm understanding. I didn't ask you if you really needed a full day off because your child had a doctor's appointment, versus asking about evening hours or if you could get an early morning or late afternoon appointment and just take a half day. So what, you are supposed to be sympathetic.

I don't ask you to get me coffee when I'm very busy or have a visitor. Damn straight.

I don't require you to stay late or come in on a weekend to finish a critical job. Hey, that's my personal time, you don't own me, I have a life of my own.

I smile a lot. Big deal.

Whoops, I forgot a card or lunch for Secretaries' Day, and besides I thought you wanted to be called Administrative Assistant. You thoughtless lout.

Whoops, I was in a rush and forgot to say thank you. You thoughtless lout.

Whoops, when you were late with the report I needed, I forgot to smile. You thoughtless lout.

On the other hand, if I took them for a nice lunch for Secretary's Day (correction: Administrative Assistant's Day! Correction: Administrative Professionals Day!), or gave them gift certificates for an expensive shop for Christmas, or spontaneously bought little floral bouquets for their desks, I was really a great guy . . . at least until my next failing.

Lest you think me contemptuous of non-exempts, I refer you back to "Delegate, Delegate, Delegate." They are neglected as a valuable resource and are underutilized. They appreciate added responsibilities and the opportunity to learn and grow. I had several male and female assistants whom I was pleased to promote to professional status. I too was a non-exempt lab assistant for seven years, starting at "level one," before securing a degree in chemistry and professional status.

Once I wrote the formal research report for a project and was told that under company policy, as a non-exempt, I was not allowed to possess a copy of it. After asking if I should burn the manuscript and erase my brain, I got a copy. And the first time someone called me "Sir," I turned around to see who was standing behind me.

5. THINKERS & NON-THINKERS

There are two types of people in the world—the thinkers and the non-thinkers. The happy ones are the non-thinkers. They float downstream like happy tubers on a hot summer's day, laughing and splashing as they drink their beers and drift along enjoying each other's small talk and jokes. Happy to be alive, happy for each other's company, happy to be away from their boring work, happy to be disconnected for a period of time. They expect little from life, do what others expect them to do, and revel in routine and security. Their brains are in beautiful condition, good as new, non-convoluted by troublesome thoughts. They expect nothing beyond working, marrying, raising children, and expiring. They really don't think about death until they are dying, when they are deeply consoled by the standard platitudes. These people have accepted the religion, and likely politics, handed to them by their parents, or negotiated with their selected mates.

The thinkers are usually unhappy. They see many problems, likely far more than actually exist, and certainly more than they will actually attempt to deal with. When all is said and done, there will be a lot more said than done. They are divided into three classes: Whiners, Bitchers, and Doers.

Whiners are the most constantly unhappy, as they dwell in negative land at all times. They tend to be lonely, because most people find them annoying. Sometimes they discover another whiner with whom to partner. This allows them to resonate and achieve super nadirs, but with some frustration in the struggle to exceed each other's lows. Sometimes they partner with a sadist, resulting in a sick, but satisfying, stable relationship. The whiner has some real ills to deal with, and the sadist has a weakling conveniently at hand to pummel, physically or verbally.

Bitchers have an endless list of inequities and conspiracies they see everywhere. The best feature of these people is that many of them are good effective workers and, unlike the whiners, accomplish a great deal. Moreover, some of their gripes have genuine merit. Thus, they often contribute to progress by not accepting the status quo too readily. They can be the bad apple in the barrel: however, others quickly identify them and discount their complaints, so long as they continue to pull the load. They certainly do not "whistle while they work."

Doers are the most vexed group, because they feel compelled to attempt to fix the wrongs they observe and contribute to what they perceive to be progress. Their constitutions will not allow them to accept the status quo, they cannot be fully obedient, docile, inactive, yes-persons, or unquestionably loyal to any cause, group, or institution. The apostle Thomas and Galileo come to mind.

They cannot escape their brains, save for very brief periods—perhaps induced by watching a fireplace, floating on the ocean, listening to great music, immersing themselves in fine literature, perhaps aided by some superior form of ethanol. But, they quickly relapse into high brain activity which they cannot switch off. Even as they sleep, their gray computers are processing data on the problems they could not solve while conscious. Frequently, they are surprised when the answer is printed out on a mental ticker tape when they awake.

Their only salvation lies in priority setting, with lists divided into, "Must Do", "Ought To Do", and "Would Be Nice To Do". Usually their heads add new items to the "Must Do" column at such a rate as to preclude much progress on the others. People who do not suffer from hyper mental efforts might regard them as self absorbed or aloof. Actually, they are capable of great compassion, but they are more likely to respond by helping people to help themselves, than by a warm hug. They are also capable of great passion when some cause, idea, or person finally manages to break through their web of glia cells and synapses to suspend rationality.

These people are the movers, shakers, and authors of art, science, business, and progress in the world. They are to be admired and pitied. I say "pitied" because they struggle against daunting odds to accomplish something new and different, which is anathema to the people surrounding them. "New and different" are things that most people like to talk about in the abstract and dread to face in the concrete, because they mean **change**. Substitute a "c" for the "g", and you have "chance", a terrorizing term. A "chance" to win a million for a buck in a lottery is fine. A chance that your idea or dream may fail and all will see it—horrors! A chance that you must leave your comfortable groove (which in reality will become a deep rut as you continue to circle the same old track) of knowns to risk failure dealing with unknowns—unthinkable.

Medicine was the backward science, relative to mathematics, physics, astronomy, and chemistry, for hundreds of years not just because of the complexities of human life, but because it was the exclusive province of medical doctors. With sincere apologies to the few Drs. Erlich, Jenner, Sabin, and Salk (Pasteur was a chemist who was derided by the French medical establishment), it only began to race when invaded by microbiologists, geneticists, and other scientists who were trained to think outside the box and search for the new—not work from rote teachings.

The Doers are not to be pitied just because they lead mentally tortured lives, not just because they struggle endlessly against obstacles and snares placed in their paths by a hidden superior intellect, and the greatest force in the universe . . . inertia. Not just because they live surrounded by a Greek Chorus chanting, "It will never work", not just because they must fail many more times than succeed, not just because they are regarded as odd by the vast majority, but because of the secret fate that awaits them. After all the impossible problems they have solved, after they have finally rolled that boulder to the top of the hill after seeing it roll back down many times, they discover that their moment of triumph is not a feeling of exultation . . . but is more akin to having a good B.M. after a period of constipation.

6. A NON-PC LOOK AT REJECTION

Women—been rejected? Get used to it. I would take odds that your professors did not address this topic in your business courses, and you'd be sentenced to an HR penal colony (or the unemployment line) if it came up at the water cooler. My career spanned the many iterations of gender-equality legislation and changing social roles, and all I ever really wanted was a solid business team and a positive bottom line. Whether the players used the men's room or the women's room was beside the point. I worked with many women at graduate levels—PhD chemists, microbiologists, mathematicians, lawyers, MBA's, etc.—who were highly experienced at dealing with rejection, as I was. I did, however, notice a gender-based difference in an employee's ability to deal with rejection at professional entry levels. Women (in general, and remember what Mark Twain said about generalities), had more problems with it than men. Men learn about rejection from their early days. We hear that boys are made from puppy dog tails and snails, while girls are made from sugar and spice, and everything nice. Having had two older brothers, two younger sisters and two daughters, I heartily subscribe.

At young ages boys are told, "Get up, you're not hurt bad, walk it off, get back in there, you're not bleeding much." Later on, they hear, "You lost the flip so you have to take Stinky on your team—we don't want him." Or the baseball coach says, "You moron, how many times do I have to tell you not to throw behind the runner?" They then progress to, "Would you care to dance?" . . ."Get lost creep." Or an all-time favorite, "Are you busy Friday night? I have reservations for dinner at Le Bec Fin, then tickets to the Philadelphia Orchestra, and we could go to a club afterward . . .". "Sorry, I have to catch up on my Tivo'ed Survivior episodes."

In contrast, when one of my daughters fell, physically or emotionally, I would be right there to dust them off, cuddle Daddy's little princess, and assure them that they were safe from the nasty world. Did I unintentionally do them a disservice when they entered their chosen fields of advertising and law, both fraught with minefields of rejection? Perhaps, though I also made a conscious effort to toughen them up when opportunities arose regarding school, sports and relationships.

Early on, we hired many women who typically had a B.S. in Chemistry or Chemical Engineering, and sent them out as sales trainees. They spent six months of product and technology training and sales training in the office. Typically they went to district offices at large cities, with a good district manager and fellow sales people. They had high salaries, new cars and expense accounts. There was little overnight travel. Most of them threw in the towel in less than two years. Our success rate at making them "Road Warriors" was very low. I attributed this phenomenon to their inability or unwillingness to deal with consistent rejection, an intrinsic part of the sales function.

If you don't possess a naturally-thick skin, or if you haven't developed adequate calluses growing up or during your education or early employment experiences, now is the time to recognize that and refocus your outlook. Your attitude must be "I'm good. I'm working hard to gain your respect and business, and if you want me out of here, you are going to have to throw me out!" Even in your first professional position, as you navigate through feeling the effects of "imposter syndrome" and gather the experience that will make you a more valuable employee down the road, you need to make a conscious decision not to take each rejection as a divine judgment that you are not up to the task and will not succeed in your profession.

Suck it up, walk it off, and persevere. I have been rejected or insulted so many times by people who were truly experts at it, that I am sure I would survive the bite of the black mamba.

7. GETTING VALUE FROM OUTSIDE DIRECTORS—
A MINI-CASE STUDY

In the past, independent directors were typically friends and associates of the principal shareholders of the company. They were not expected to do much and mainly offered their credibility. They often sat on the boards of many other companies. More recently, however, a great deal of attention has been focused on what independent directors are supposed to do—provide a governance and ethics function independent of the interests of stakeholders. Consider my experience as a case study.

I had a fair amount of contact with outside directors at a Fortune 500 global company and have also served as an outside director during a six-year stint on the board of a midsize specialty manufacturing firm. At the major firm, many of the "outside" directors were sycophants, cronies, celebrities, or academics, who had not a clue about the real world business. I had no idea of their expected contributions, and nor did they. Those who had labored in allied industries, or had extensive special knowledge in law, finance, international dealings, research, marketing, etc., were the only ones of real value to the operation.

In contrast, I was impressed with the high value that the smaller firm extracted from their outside directors. This firm, which was growing at an impressive rate, had three inside directors who, as shareholders in the S-corporation, were vitally committed to the growth and profitability of the business. The three outside directors typically served for six years (at the discretion of the shareholders), on a rotating basis á la the U.S. Senate. This method allowed the directors to gain deep knowledge of the business and personnel, but permitted the entrance of fresh blood and views. In turn, these new perspectives could be meshed with the evolving needs of the firm and prevent diminishing returns from the "outs." The outs were paid flat fees for their service, and were immune from financial concerns with stock valuation. They were free to speak frankly with the "ins" and the CEO in private group sessions following the quarterly meetings, at which managers had presented their results and plans.

The dialogue was always civil, but also quite frank. None of the outs felt financial pressure to sugarcoat their views and the ins were mature enough to absorb their comments and suggestions even when faces were slightly red. I was delighted to speak and hear direct talk about real business issues.

When I arrived, the senior out had been the CEO of a mid-sized steel firm and had experienced everything from the salad days through the world glut of steel to the eventual bankruptcy of his firm. Mere recessions did not frighten him and he gave expert advice for ways to survive in a down market.

The other out had a wide background in general management and could offer sage suggestions, in delicately-fashioned words. He was absolutely critical in negotiating the acquisition of a smaller German firm, where the former owner's retention was key to easing the integration process. He detected their unstated concern that their firm would be stripped down. He assured them that in all of his service with the acquiring company, he had never seen the shareholders attempt to milk the assets, but rather always acted from a desire to grow the enterprise.

I arrived with P&L experience for a major business in a highly-allied industry, focused on research, market development, and joint ventures with foreign firms. On my first walk through of their production plants I noticed that they were using large quantities of a highly volatile organic solvent and spotted a pager hanging from a worker's belt. A sparking device! They quickly adopted new safety regulations, and I pressed them to store back-up business data off-site, and have an emergency plan in hand against the possible loss of a production unit. I also urged them to improve margins by forcing productivity improvement by rigidly controlling complement.

In my early days, I found that they were suffering from "ANALYSIS PARALYSIS". As a former artillery fire direction computer (pre-GPS), I realized that it is critical to know where you are before trying to shoot at distant invisible targets. However, they were overdoing it by slicing and dicing financial data from existing products, sold to existing customers, in existing markets, almost to the exclusion of efforts on new fronts.

I also found that virtually all of their "research" was really short range sales, and technical service, and short range minor developments. The reason for this was that they had a sales department, but no real marketing group. I pressed them to secure a topflight marketing manager. They did, and he quickly segmented the available market to direct research better, started a branding program and worked well in developing relationships with key accounts.

This progressive company treats its employees well, is growing domestically (in a consolidating industry) and is spreading its geographic coverage to Europe and Asia, while raising its profit margins. They are headed by a youngish shareholder who has developed into a fine CEO, with an excellent business planning process. A profit-sharing plan prevents employees from tolerating slackers or incompetents.

I always thought the best definition of a true professional was someone who is paid to tell you what he thinks. Firms who are willing to invest some time seeking out true professionals as outside directors, and then are smart and humble enough to use them wisely, will maximize the value derived from this often underutilized resource. Rubber stamps are just too pliable to be an effective tool on your boards.

Chapter 4

Nuts and Bolts

1 (a). FINANCE: ON FINANCE

There are good reasons to know hard financial numbers on the value of your firm. First of all, from the obvious legal standpoint, if you have any stock on the market, your fiduciary duties can strip you of your personal fortunes or put you in jail if the firm is engaged in creative accounting.

The second reason, and actually the primary one from a business standpoint, is to have an *accurate* measure of how the firm is really doing. In the artillery, the first thing I learned was that you could not shoot at distant targets if you didn't know where the hell you were. A crude pick-off by a good map reader could get you started for area fire, but until the survey team arrived with decimal point location (global positioning satellites sure would have been handy), we couldn't shoot precision targets or lay them in within 50 yards of our own troops. The other part of this, one of the great laws of science, is that you can't be really effective until you can measure something accurately. Ergo, we have dynes, ergs, joules, nanoseconds etc., and the progress from the sundial to the atomic clock.[6]

Profit numbers can be moved all over the place by selective actions, and revenues can be boosted by special sales promotions and discounts, but if you can show that the net worth of the company is increasing, hopefully at an

---

[6]   If you get a chance to catch the movie "Longitude" you'll see that prior to the early 1800's, thousands of sailors were lost at sea for lack of an accurate clock.

accelerating rate, faster than inflation, then you are making **real measurable progress**. Most of the growth can be attained by acquisitions, but margin growth must be obtained by superior marketing or research.

1(b). FINANCE: MEASURES OF PROFITABILITY— KEY RATIOS

Financial people are critical to your success, but they can also be dangerous to the business. They should serve, but not lead, the business. I have seen them "save" firms out of business. It is crucial to understand their lingo and ratios, but make your decisions based on **your** knowledge of your customers, your market and your competitors. Here is a thumbnail sketch of some key financial ratios with which you can gauge some real information about the financial health of your concern.

1. Earnings Per Share

Net Income ÷ Shares Outstanding = EPS

This equation is used to compare one year's earnings with those of prior years. Extraordinary income/losses are noted in the annual report to assist in understanding any fluctuations.

2. Return on Common Equity

Net Income ÷ Common Equity = RCE

Example: $5,400/$46,500 = 11.6% RCE

This figure is used to compare how a firm stands vis-à-vis other firms in the industry. Judgment must be exercised since income might be affected by new investment (higher depreciation) and sales expenses associated with promoting new products, etc.

3. Return on Assets and the Leverage Effect

$$\frac{\textit{Earnings—Interest}}{\text{Total Assets—Debt}} = \text{ROA}$$

Example: $\dfrac{\$11 - \$2}{\$100 - \$40}$ = 15% ROA

Return on common equity is a consequence of two factors:

a. Return on assets
b. The extent to which leverage is employed.

Suppose, for example, the firm has obtained 40% of its capital ($40) by borrowing at an interest rate of 5% ($2 per year). The ROA as noted in the example above is 15%. This is successful leverage since the 5% borrowing rate of interest is less than the overall earnings rate on capital employed (11%).

4. Return on Net Assets

RONA = Asset Turnover x OPAT (Operating Profit after Taxes) Margin
= Sales/Net Assets x Income/Sales

RONA is a consequence of asset turnover and profit margin. If profit margins cannot be improved, then a higher turnover rate (especially in inventory levels where a market manager has some leverage) must be achieved to increase return.

5. Coverage Ratio

$$\frac{\text{Earnings before interest and taxes}}{\text{Investment}} = \text{Coverage Ratio}$$

A firm's earnings must cover its interest charges to maintain a solvent position. This argument can be extended to other fixed obligations, such as management salaries, fringe benefits, etc. that would not shrink automatically when sales take a massive downturn. As a general rule, the higher the earnings volatility, the higher should be the coverage ratio.

6. Liquidity Ratio

Current Assets ÷ Current Liabilities = Liquidity Ratio
The term "current" is generally defined as one year. The lower the ratio, the more difficult it would be for a firm to borrow money or to purchase goods. This ratio is a guide for credit departments to approve sales.

7. Receivables Turnover

Sales ÷ Receivables = Receivables Turnover

Example: $105,200 ÷ $19,800 = 5.3 times

Another method in understanding this statistic is the "collection period" or number of days that sales are outstanding. This is computed as follows:

Sales ÷ 360 = Average daily sales

Example: $105,200 ÷ 360 = $292.22 Average daily sales

Receivables ÷ Average daily sales = Number of days

Example: $19,800 ÷ $292.22 = 68 days

The above are regarded as indications of:

Liquidity of receivables.

Quality of receivables

Firm's credit-granting policies

Receivables are an investment and low turnover has a direct impact on RONA.

8. Inventory Turnover

Sales ÷ Inventories = Inventory Turnover

$105,200 ÷ 35,900 = 2.9 times

A low ratio is indicative of slow-moving inventory. A falling ratio is indicative of a drop in liquidity, high carrying costs and possible losses from obsolescence. Again, inventory is an investment and low turnover has a direct impact on RONA.

I once had a V.P. of Finance tell me that our corporation rested on a three—legged stool of stockholders' return, debt/equity ratio, and RONA. I responded that the company got off its ass by seeking out a market need, developing a product to fill the need uniquely well, and pricing it to the nibs. If we were successful in that, all the financial ratios would look good. If we weren't, we would descend into becoming a commodity chemical company.

Financial people can always show you how to avoid risk and save money by not investing in "newness". Of course your business is heading down the escalator as you stand still, and your competitors are stepping over you to make the climb.

1(c). FINANCE: SOME MORE FINANCIALS

Recall that RONA = OPAT x ASSET TURNOVERS. This equation tells you how efficiently the assets are being utilized. It is affected by pricing, costs, plant performance, collections, inventory, investment, depreciation, etc.

The Debt to Equity Ratio tells you the level of risk that is being assumed to generate the profits. Two companies could both have 10% RONAS, one at a D/E ratio of 5 and the other at 0.5 (which causes stockholders to sleep better). Of course if the 5 company is expanding its plants and revenues rapidly, it could well be worth the risks. However, if it is borrowing money to buy dot com stocks on margin . . . it is heading for a disaster that will leave its stockholders naked. Obviously when you make an acquisition the D/E ratio climbs, but there should be a target range for the corporation.

Regarding the return to shareholders, if you aren't making more than government bonds, why bear the risks of business?

Always take anything I say about financial matters with a full salt shaker, and remember my motto—frequently wrong, never in doubt. That said, I think that D/E for a solid manufacturing firm should be in the range of 50%—much less than that and you might be sitting on your fannies, much higher—you might be playing with matches.

A rule of thumb for gross profits for manufacturers is—

> 20% Gross Profit—Treading Water.
> 30% Gross Profit—Good Business
> 40% Gross Profit—Fine Business—but tough to attain unless you
> have super technology or are the lowest cost producer.

A well-run, good marketing outfit should be able to get in the 30's—which would produce excellent RONA's.

2(a). PRICING: PRICING THEORY AND PRACTICE

You might have learned to construct a revenue curve by plotting the amount of product sales you get at various prices and laying it over a plot of fixed and variable costs, similar to my artistic rendering below. This is all a crock in the real world, as I never got enough data to construct a revenue curve, but it is of great value to understand the built-in mindsets and battles between sales and marketing, entrepreneur and finance, finance and research, etc.

Sales and entrepreneurs want to price for greatest revenue (Point A). Unfortunately, it is the higher price which reduces the amount sold, but which yields the greatest distance between the cost line and the revenue curve, which yields the greatest profit (Point B).

Finance wants the greatest profit, as does marketing, but they feud over *risks*. Marketing wants to assume more risk, as does research, but finance cannot calculate a return on investment on a new venture, an idea, or a researcher's brain.

Research always says "I think I can do this." Marketing has to say, "I know you can—given unlimited time and money, but can we afford to have you do it?"

In the end, the price of anything is what the market will bear. Finding that price is like descending a staircase in pitch blackness and feeling with your foot for the next step—which you hope is there. Note that a major firm recently overpriced their new cell phones by $100. Of course it is easier to go down when you mis-price and it is a bitch to try to go up.

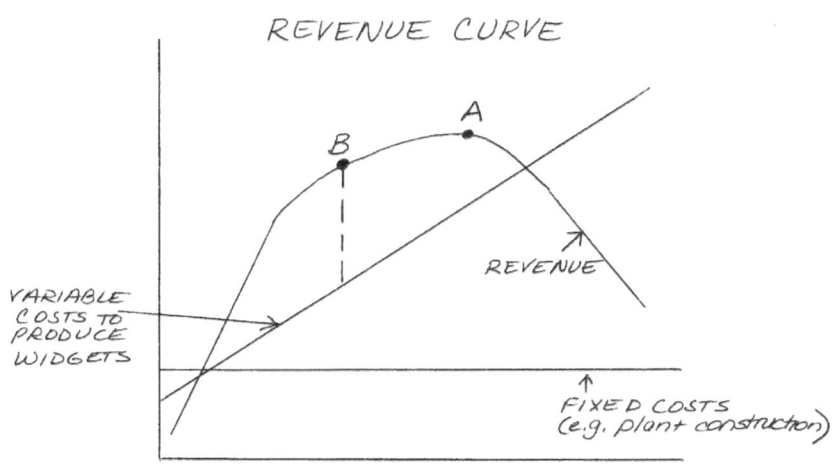

REVENUE CURVE

Units of Widgets Sold

2(b). PRICING: PRICING TACTICS

Maintain a price list of standard products at standard [high] prices. Give **volume** discounts if you must, in the form of quarterly rebates, but invoice at list price. This lets you keep the money a little longer, makes the head of purchasing a star four times a year, keeps the real price on a need-to-know basis, and maybe fogs up competitors a little. An important legal point is that you must offer the same volume discount to all customers for the same product who qualify. Make **value engineered** versions of standard products, i.e., you find a way to make the standard product a little cheaper or faster or maybe even not quite as good. It can be offered to customers of your choosing at a lower price, which gives them a feeling of having a preferred position. I had one value-engineered product that I sold to a dozen major accounts, and it did not have to appear on our price list. Again, a legal caveat is that if another customer were to learn of the product and ask for it, you would be obligated to sell it to them at the same price.

Some valuable pricing tactics include:

Custom Products—These are reserved for big volume. You can design a product for a single customer—or simply make a small variation on a standard product, name it for the customer (they love that) and price it wherever you like. It does not appear on the price list and does not have to be sold to anyone else.

Price Exceptions—You are free to match any competitor's price based on credible evidence that it really is what your customer is paying. It's best to have an invoice, but a letter from the purchasing agent is good enough. If you are daring, you may accept an oral statement from an executive. If you do this, write a call report or memo giving the date, time, and location of the conversation and file it carefully. Better yet, write a self-serving letter to the customer and note that the price you have quoted is in response to the competitive situation you discussed.

Quarterly Price—Another device that worked well for my business was to give customers contracts with quarterly "price notification" clauses (not "price protection", which may have some legal problems). The business had a fair amount of seasonality, with the first and second quarters dominating. Thus I could "predict" to customers in the fourth quarter, *before* they prepared their business plans for the following year, that I might have to go up as much as 5%, as early as the first quarter. When, in fact, price increases of 4% were announced in mid-April, they would not have to pay it until the end of June. This gave them a tail-wind favorable surprise in achieving their business plans. Of course, I was set up to achieve my profit gains for the next year. Also, I could hardly be charged with illegally signaling my competitors of price increases, when my forecasts were incorrect.

Claim Settlements with Customers—These can actually be a chance to lock up business for a period of time or to gain additional sales. One way to accomplish this is to pay the claim by a discount on future purchases. The customer must stay with you to get the money, which the customer sees as the market-value of the product, but which you see as the much lower cost of the goods.

In addition, you might be able to give them motivation to place purchases of other materials with you. In one case I handled, the claim was based on our sales of trade sales polymers to a firm which captively made large quantities of industrial coatings polymers. They purchased large quantities of monomers from competitors of our firm, so we offered a discount on monomer sales so they could get their claim settled faster. In effect our monomer competitors were paying part of the claim against us.

It would be a good idea to run these tactics past your lawyer before you use any of them. Only stupid people lie to their doctor, lawyer, or tax-accountant. I can make a pretty good case for lying on occasion to just about anyone else, other than a customer.

2(c). PRICING: THE ART OF PRICE INCREASES

Suppose that your suppliers' prices went up 3%, and your firm matched the increases for your customers. We could call that pretty good and move on, but clear opportunities to raise prices have been very scarce the last few years and should be exploited to the max. I suggest you could have gotten more. Pick an odd number, so it looks like it was carefully calculated and represents an effort to hold the line . . . say 4.3%.

Then you roll it out, as follows:

> "Valued customers, we regret that we find it necessary to raise our prices by 4.3%, effective some date. This is a reflection of higher raw material prices precipitated by the run up in oil and energy prices, the cost of complying with government regulations on pollution and other items, and salary creep precipitated by the extremely tight labor market with the need to attract and retain highly skilled professionals, who are required to enable us to meet your needs for high-quality, innovative, well-supplied and serviced products. We will continue to strive to meet and exceed your demands for improved products and service via research developments and through our ambitious active programs, to improve our quality and service constantly, so that we contribute real value to you. We want to earn your business every day."

The difference between 4.3 and 3.0 is only $13,000.00 per $MM, but when you multiply that by many millions of sales, it amounts to many dollars of profit—pure profit! You would have to secure a number of $MM's in additional sales to generate that profit otherwise. Plus, once you have this extra gravy, you can start to multiply it by the number of years. Do a price increase every few years and it is a big deal. Of course you must be prepared to cut deals with a few accounts to prevent any sizeable volume loss, but these are usually minor ego satisfiers for purchasing directors to show their management skills. I used to pilot price increases by making personal phone calls to the toughest purchasing managers I knew as the announcement letters were being mailed.

Pricing is an art, but you know you have it about right when everyone is at least a little irritated with you; your sales and marketing people and customers grumble. And still, your own management and research people ask "Is that all you're getting?"

A little boy went into a candy shop to buy a chocolate rabbit, but when the clerk handed it to him, he turned it over and closely observed the area between the hind legs. He handed it back to the clerk and said, "This is a female rabbit, I want a male one." The clerk said, "There is a very small difference between them." The boy responded, "Yes, but it is all chocolate."

2(d). PRICING: COPPER PRICES

I have been asked why I follow copper prices so closely. I use the Dow-Jones as a leading indicator for what is likely to happen in 6-9 months, unemployment as a laggard telling you what happened about six months or more in the past, new housing starts as a closer in leader, the index of industrial production (now known as the I.S.M.—Index of Supply Management) as a coincidental indicator for industrial production, paper board as a close in leader (boxes for those widgets), and, yes, copper prices as a slight laggard for industrial production. The Basis? You can't build a house or car without copper wire. Also, when industrial products are selling, think of all the copper windings in all the little electric motors for washing machines, dryers, air conditioners, fans, dishwashers, etc., not to mention copper tubing, drills, pumps, and so on. There is an old saying, "Every bull market has a copper roof."

3(a). PRODUCIVITY: MIS AND COMPUTERS

"Where's The Beef?" If you remember the old hamburger ad, wherein a firm extolled all of its virtues in serving the public, and an old lady dissatisfied customer kept asking "Where's the beef?" . . . that is what I'm doing. I once attended a board meeting at which a fellow outside director noted that there had been no reduction in the breakeven point and that the firm still required the same monthly sales. This despite the many glowing reports on the computer accounting management system by articulate, intelligent, sincere young employees telling of its wonders. Everyone knows "that" is the right thing to do, but no one can demonstrate a real measurable pay-off. This is not new to me. I used to be assessed three times the number of dollars I had spent with advertising, promotion, technical literature, and absolutely invaluable customers at trade shows each year for "MIS" (management information services), which endeavored to drown me in IBM sheets every week. They were chock full of data I did not need but the department could never answer a question that would have helped me run my business better. I believe that they existed to make graphs for the VP's and the Board.[7]

Very early on I had our exposure panels (> 40,000 panels in various locations) computerized and purchased 45 pc's for our field reps. I also hired the first "information technology" professional for our business team. She proved highly valuable at tracking competitors and their plants via literature searches and exploiting government filings for permits for building, waste, etc. Still, we had to buy PC's, train our own people and develop the programs to yield data which would be useful. I'll disclaim up-front my dinosaur status on the entire world of computers, but hear me out on this one.

Up to 1991 when I retired, my firm had spent about $200 million on main frames, PC's and MIS, which occupied more office space than the two largest businesses in the corporation. This space was filled with high-priced people

---

[7]   At one point I became the research manager for three different businesses (Coatings, Textile and Paper, and Leather), which had been combined into a new department. I needed a report to collate all of their expenses for sales and technical service, after I provided single definitions to employ. I met with MIS and was told that it would cost at least $250,000 (in 1980 dollars), and take six months to develop. I said "no thanks." Two weeks later, a subordinate walked into my office and tossed the required program on my desk, noting that he had created it in his spare time! This employee, Jim Gambino, was one of the brightest and most creative people I ever met. A few years later he rightly left our company to accept a VP position with another major firm.

who never conceived, developed, produced, marketed, or sold a product, or defeated a competitor. There had been no measurable improvement in productivity.

I also discovered that some people drowned themselves in data to the point where they lost their originality. Schopenhauer wrote an essay about educated people who had "read themselves stupid" on a topic.[5] Researchers at Cornell and Stanford recently concluded that the use of computers and the Internet had led toward scientifically-measurable cognitive losses, in the form of shallower thinking.[6] These findings echo Roman Philosopher Seneca's 2000 year-old observation that "To be everywhere is to be nowhere."[7]

Naturally PC's can be useful for businesses. They must, however, be in the hands of highly-trained personnel, who first must really understand the business, so that they can write programs that will actually aid the business, versus trying to shoe-horn the business into an existing program. Data input has to be severely restricted to slow the rate of pollution of the data base. I believe, however, that the costs of developing these systems are grossly underestimated. If you had issued a charge number to be assigned to all efforts on BAAN, it would likely knock your hat off.

The real pay-off must come via improved productivity.[8] The best way of insuring this is to sit rigidly on complement while driving up revenues, numbers of customers, margins, and geographical coverage. While complement remains constant, I would hope to see a shift in numbers from administration toward marketing/sales with an ensuing increase in research.

My challenge to a firm is, "Put your productivity where your mouth is." Let's see some real measurable results such as, increased sales and profits per employee, gross profit margins, etc. I will note that I enjoy setting goals for others, while giving them the freedom to work out the details.

---

8   A family lawyer was invited to the wedding of a client's daughter. Two weeks later she came to his office in tears, explaining that her new husband was impotent. He offered his sympathy and assured her that he would quickly obtain an annulment. The following year he again attended a wedding for the young woman. A month later she returned in tears after discovering that her groom was gay (*another* annulment). The next year, with trepidation, he attended her third wedding. Six months passed by and he met her on the street. She was in high spirits and smiling. He congratulated her that she had finally found a satisfying relationship and gotten her sex life squared away. She commented that she and her new husband had not actually had sex yet. But, she was very happy, because her husband was a computer expert and he explained how great it was going to be!

3(b). PRODUCIVITY: PRODUCT LINE RATIONALIZATION

Some firms end up with *too many* products and could benefit from a rationalization, likely resulting in more profits, not less, and improved customer service and relationships, not worse. It would certainly improve plant performance. I lived and learned through one of these, wherein the line was trimmed from 900 down to 750. The reason rationalizations become necessary is that the greatest force in the universe is inertia. To paraphrase Sir Isaac Newton, "Bodies at rest or in motion, remain at rest or in motion, until they are acted upon by an external force."

Product line rationalization doesn't take rocket science or a massive accounting exercise, but it does take a solid management commitment, and a tough, knowledgeable, persistent, project leader—working against a firm completion date. It is even better if the effort would benefit the project leader directly, such as a production manager.

The mechanism you use can be a simple ranking of products from top to bottom for revenue, and supposed profit contribution. Single year effects should be considered as well as developmental status. Next draw a bold line across the list. This is not an exercise to eliminate a few obvious old dogs, but should be an effort to truly streamline the offerings. There should be some howls of pain at the initial cut, most likely from sales and marketing, and later from some customers when a final list is proffered. Work can be directed at considering product substitution recommendations. Then you can engage in a real open debate about where the line is drawn, considering factors such as customer leverage, which should be genuinely tested and not assumed.

Customer objections can be handled in a variety of fashions, ranging from simply saying, "I'm sorry but the material will no longer be available past [some future date]" to caving in. If you have to capitulate to protect a major account, you can sell it as a positive for your firm responding to the customer's needs. At the other end, you may find a customer has been unable to find a substitute and you may graciously agree to "custom" supply the product. Naturally this accommodation would come with a much higher price tag and perhaps a requirement that you can only do it if the customer buys an annual quantity in a single production run, preferably at year end so the inventory costs go on the customer's books instead of yours.

Product line rationalization should give a boost to your quality and service efforts, reduce plant and inventory costs, and relieve strain on all functions, including purchasing, billing, and credit. It will help ensure that there is no wasted sales or technical service time on piss ant products, and make people think bigger when considering new targets from customers and research.

3(c). PRODUCIVITY: PRODUCT LINE CHURN

Product line churn can become a concern to your financial people and others. It has to be built into your plans, and is one more reason that "standing still" will kill your business. A typical manufacturing firm must expect a lot of this, because many items cannot be patented, are possible to reverse engineer, or, if the volume becomes large and is a significant cost item to the customer, become part of captive manufacture. Of course competitors will be attracted, and the customer's purchasing people will be out fishing.

As Satchel Paige once said of his advancing age as a pitcher, "Don't look back. Something might be gaining on you."[8] You need a lively marketing group searching out new developments targets, at larger volumes, and courting your larger existing accounts. When your products tend to be small (but critical) items in a complex, expensive assembly, such as aerospace, you have some insurance. But there is no way you can bottom feed!

Chapter 5

Where Do You Go From Here?

1. ACQUISITIONS

I recently read an article regarding RPM International Inc., which represented a "lucky break", "fortuitous happenstance", or "serendipity" (these terms represent my progression over the years).[9] It exactly reinforces what I advocate—growth through acquisitions by a small company who has its own act together and where "good enough" is not accepted as good enough.

When I first got involved in the Coatings Industry, there were 1800 companies. When I left there were fewer than 800. Valspar is a good example of a smaller concern that grew into a major by a process of acquisitions and consolidation. Here is another one, RPM. When I first dealt with Republic Powdered Metals in the 60's, it was a small supplier of specialty industrial coatings. It went from $11 MM in sales in 1971 to $2 BILLION in 2001!!! That deserves multiple exclamation points. They now own DAP (a major independent and private labeler of caulks, sealants, and adhesives), Zinnser (noted for specialty primers and stain blockers), and Rust-Oleum (corrosion inhibiting paints). Interestingly, these are all items which paint companies can manufacture for themselves, but frequently buy and re-sell in their own stores.

I believe that this topic deserves serious attention and discussion in *truly long range planning*. Obviously, you have to be satisfied that your base is solid, and that you are one of those greater than 1.0 "SO-SO" companies before you can do more than think and talk about it.

Your firm should have a policy on this topic, because on the positive side, acquisitions provide a route to growth and earnings. On the negative side, the wrong acquisitions can lead to the destruction of the corporation. An acquisition is like two porcupines making love. If it is done carefully, it can be mutually gratifying—otherwise you just get pricked. Even if your firm has not yet become the "OPTIMA" corporation, but is on sound footing and has progressed beyond the "SO-SO" firm level, you need to consider growth via acquisitions and feasting on competitors' mistakes and failings.

This blurb is certainly not a detailed road map, but it does represent a philosophy. One key item is the concept that growth should be built outward like a coral reef, not jumping far afield from internal knowledge and experience, and then trying to link the islands.

"I am the second kimono from the left, after
consuming the required amount of sake."

"This is one fellow I never disagreed with in Japan."

2. JOINT VENTURES/PARTNERSHIPS/MERGERS

The marriage of two firms must meet the three key criteria for any cooperative effort:

1. Good Will
2. Mutual Benefit
3. Capability of both partners to perform

If either partner wants to go into a relationship with the objective of doing in the other, and they are willing to lie, cheat, and steal, they will likely be successful in doing so. Lawyers can't write enough whereas's and whereby's to protect you fully, just enough to limit the damage. It is absolutely key that both parties trust each other fully and that involves the usual courtship phase. If there is an element of distrust by one partner, it will be *detected* and *reflected* by the other and begin to poison the relationship. Unfortunately, a little bit of strychnine is fatal. Truly, if it doesn't feel good, *don't do it*. Of course a "win-win" outcome must be apparent, and both partners must bring genuine strength to the effort. One strong partner and one weak partner, or two weak partners, will not succeed in a profitable ongoing relationship.

I believe that the contribution of each partner must represent a true complementary marriage and not be based solely on money. While I am not one to belittle money, it is not enough to hold together a trying relationship because it is too commodity like and, of itself, does not generate respect. I believe that the approach of diversifying solely on the basis of having some cash to invest, coupled with the cavalier belief that someone else's business is "easy" to learn if you are steeped in basic management skills, was the source of the largely unsuccessful diversification programs of the 1970's and 80's. It possibly also spawned the idea that Robert McNamara could run the Department of Defense because he was a success at running Ford. The tendency now to build on some basic strength and bring the firms together in a complementary fashion will lead to a higher success rate. The following figures illustrate the situation graphically:

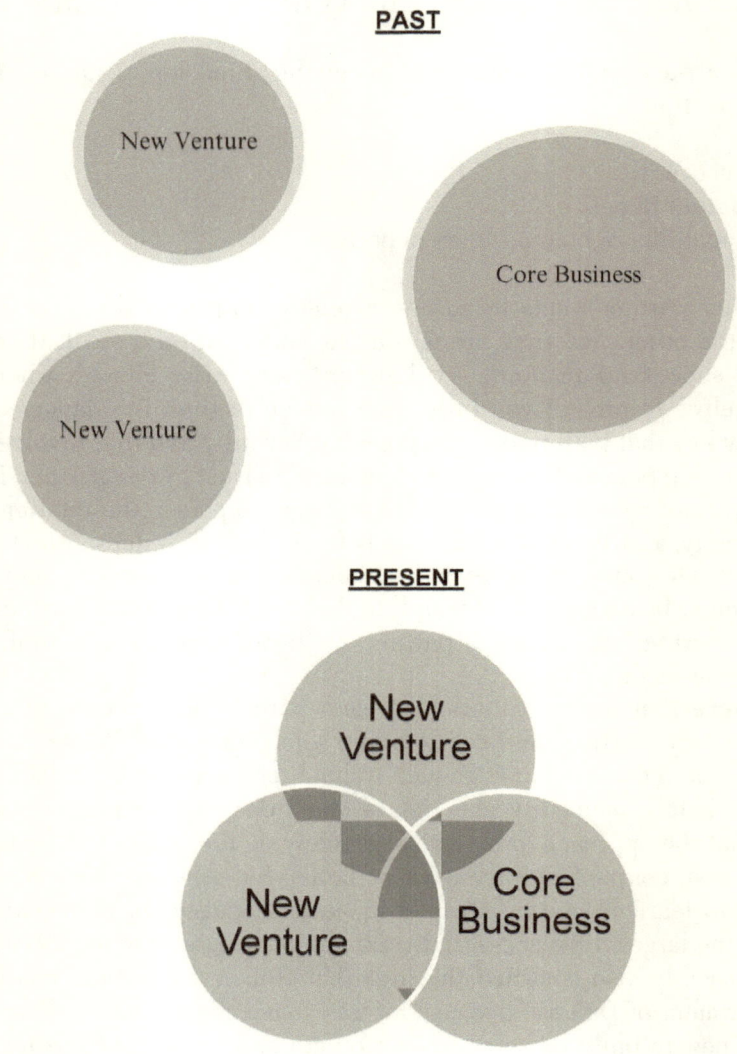

Our Japanese partners had ongoing relations with their customers, who were moving into the U.S. and Europe. My firm already had an infrastructure in North America and Europe and a strong complementary research and market development program in the same areas. These were ideal conditions for forming a joint venture.

While it might not be critical, a fourth beneficial factor in forming a successful joint venture is when each party has a good sense of humor. No matter how carefully you plan, problems will appear as soon as you start. It has occurred to me that the same requirements are necessary for a marriage. Mine has worked for 53 years thus far, even though I only have a 0.5 sense of humor. Fortunately for me, my wife has a complementary 1.5.

If the basic requirements are apparent, then it is possible to go ahead in a fashion such as:

1. *Agreed Basic Vision*—Where do you want the venture to end up?
2. *Design Phases*—These plans should be broken down into realistic and achievable blocks of objectives with finite time lines and expense limits.
3. *Adjust, Adjust, Adjust*

Some papers have been critical of the focus on "making the deal" without considering what will be the outcome. On the other hand, it is likely that you can plan forever and not foresee the myriad of problems which will be encountered as you actually try to operate the joint venture. This is where "Good Will", a qualitative statement of a "Basic Vision" and clearly stated phases are requirements. Phases could be designated as co-distribution of existing products first, cooperative marketing and research on new product definitions and development next, co-manufacturing next, and perhaps finally, a full stand-alone joint venture company.

The "adjust" item is critical and regular meetings, likely quarterly, are highly desirable to review results and discuss plans and expenses for the next quarter. Formal signed reports are a good idea to ensure that all present "understood" the events in the same fashion. Frequently, it is useful to discuss problems at lower levels in advance of the formal meeting as "surprise" problems may be embarrassing to a partner.

A new venture must deal with risk and uncertainty and requires personal energy at a rate which would daunt many. A good tactic is to make sure that the project champions have no security blankets, i.e., their only assignment is the success of the venture—they have no other comfortable roles, duties, or routines they can slide into when the heat intensifies.

They must push, push, push. The greatest danger to newness is indifference.

3. *FUTURE RISKS*

Now that things are generally going well for your firm,[9] it is time to consider what could screw it up. As Browning put it, "Let me count the ways."

1. A falling out between partners. This is not likely because I see all necessary components for a successful marriage . . . good will, mutual benefit, two strong partners, and two good senses of humor.
2. The death of an owner without a succession plan in place.
3. A disastrous acquisition, such as a hidden problem you buy with the acquired company.
4. A major fire or plant disaster. Your firm has volatile organic solvents all over the place. Familiarity may not breed contempt, but it sometimes leads to casualness. I know from experience. I virtually bathed in acetone and was fairly casual about safety until a chemist I knew unscrewed a cap on a bottle of ether, peroxides formed in the lid, it blew glass shards into his gut, and he bled to death. What would be the effect of a major fire and explosion on your firm?
5. The potential failure of your Research Department to navigate successfully the transition from technical service to advanced product development, as required by marketing for higher margin products.
6. Loss of key personnel. I recommend that you find a way to secure the few key people who really drive the business. Consider granting bonuses of non-voting stock or some other device, which allows them to feel ownership and share in the profits.
7. Company over-expands and leverages itself too far to survive a major economic downturn.
8. Great success. The ultimate failure of a great company is great success, which brings high market share and arrogance. Arrogance leads to shrinking market share and failure. The example of General Motors comes to mind. Nothing fails like success.
9. The growth and divergence of your family. Essentially, your business is a family-run enterprise. They generally are sold out by the third or fourth generation, probably because the number of heirs goes up geometrically while the profits go up linearly. Note that John D. Rockefeller was fully as rich as Bill Gates, but by the fourth generation the Rockefellers had to sell Rockefeller Center because the family needed the money! The only exception I can think of to this observation would be the Rothschilds, who are expected to pass on more than they got.

---

[9] Though this essay assesses the state of a particular family-owned manufacturing company, the enumerated risks are typical of many firms.

4. ON WEATHERING A RECESSION

There are some good things about recessions. If the old saw about problems being opportunities in disguise is correct, recessions must be great opportunities. Managing a firm through a recession is worth more than a prestigious MBA. You learn more about the business and yourself than you ever wanted to. "When the going gets tough, the tough get going" is not a trite slogan.

Customer contact should become intense. A recession is a great time to learn more about your customers' businesses and the people themselves. Demonstrate that your reps are more than "order takers." Talk to the accounts even when you know there are no orders available, discuss their problems, give what little aid you can, commiserate, buy them a drink and **listen**. A few of them will actually remember you favorably when smooth sailing returns; they might even give you a call to alert you to a new opportunity or to developing problems. A recession is a good time for your people to learn where their paychecks come from, and that customers are not required to be lovable, but if they pay their bills, they should be loved.

Pivot points for the business are easier to discern when the roses are stripped away. A recession is the ideal time to correct the small excesses that creep in when times are good. A little wastage here, too much inventory there, a job that can be combined away, a superior replacement who becomes available because of the recession to replace the weak performer you've been tolerating, the advertisements that did not pay off, the enjoyable training courses that did not enhance performance, use of FedEx and UPS, where regular mail or faxes would suffice, etc. In toto, these can be big, as cost savings flow right to the bottom line.

Recessions do end; it just seems like they last forever. Most are over in one or two years. During the "double dip" recession of 1981 and 1982, I never worked so hard for less business. I asked every gray-haired customer "Do you remember things being worse than this?" When they all said "no," at least I knew that I was not just being paranoid.

Smile a lot and act confident. A good definition of class is having grace under pressure. Airline passengers in a plane with an engine afire want to hear a pilot with a calm voice.

5. EPILOGUE: FINAL HAAGRAM (WRITTEN DURING A RECESSION)

When the end of my term as an outside director arrived, I wrote the CEO a "summing up" memo, which follows below. Perhaps you can tap a trusted resource, such as an outside director or a mentor, to give you a frank evaluation of the "state of the company" or the "state of your performance." You should not wait for your retirement party to get this type of assessment. Consider the following:

Perhaps you are tiring a bit from carrying a heavy load and feeling the pressure from results which are always just around the corner. An acquisition is like catching a hot potato with both hands, and turning a company is like steering an ocean liner—you set the proper course, turn the wheel—and then wait and wait for the ship to respond. Your first foreign acquisition has been successfully integrated, brought to profitability and has increased your geographic coverage. It also allowed the two firms to exchange knowledge and technology, proving that cross pollination does not have to mean being screwed by strangers. Now you can do it again, again, and again.

You have done all the right and difficult things, including some tough measures, but remember that the longest journey also ends with one step. Good things lie ahead, but there will be a long list of new and odious problems in front of you. You are stuck with being a "Doer", and that will be your fate. Been there, done that. Your creation of a profit-sharing plan for your employees was excellent. The idea of a separate monthly paycheck if financial goals are met is terrific—welding your workforce to the success of the enterprise, giving them incentive to look for improvements, and making them intolerant of goof-offs and slackers.

Cheer up—things could be a hell of a lot worse if not for you. I always had a bottom line that I used several times in my career, "If you think you can do it better than I am, or if you want to put someone else in my place—do it. If not, I'm going to do it my way."

I'm standing down because your firm's needs are now more organizational, financial, and field sales—which I recognize as my weak areas. Also, you are getting into diminishing returns with me. I highly recommend that you read "Evolution and Revolution as Organizations Grow" by Larry E. Greiner.[10]

I am happy to report that your firm has a real aroma of success these days. If I could buy stock in it, I would. You have grown tremendously, and now have surrounded yourself with a first rate staff. As a boss, I always found that if I had a solid staff and kept all the Mickey Mouse distractions away from them, good things happened.

Based on my elemental knowledge of Finance, I concluded years ago that your firm needed to achieve only modest growth in volumes and margins to become a money-making machine. In fact, I challenged you to decide if you just wanted to become a "Fat Cat", or a "Tiger" via acquisitions. I am happy to report that BOD meetings now focus on ideas, marketing, and achievements, rather than being endless exercises on slicing and dicing financial data based on existing products, sold in existing markets, to existing customers. Focusing on the status quo, rather than topics which can grow the business, can lead to the disease of analysis paralysis. Yes it is important to understand costs; yes, savings flow directly to the bottom line. But you have an exceptional production manager who will assuredly find ways to lower your production times and costs, reduce off-grade and raise quality if left alone and supported. In the interim, does it really matter what column the variances are put in?

Don't let the trees obliterate the forest. When developments continue to score hits, demonstrating that you have a good process, it's time to apply them to better targets, such as bigger volumes, higher profits, and new customers and market segments. Analysis paralysis can, and does, get in the way of forward actions.

Spend your energy to get a top VP for sales and marketing NOW! Improve your geographical coverage NOW! Spend your time in these areas NOW! Team building is good, team leading is critical. Not everyone has to be on your team, nor should you want everyone on your team. If someone won't sign up or can't perform, or resists the direction you have selected, send them back to the minors.

Some of your direct reports seem too casual about follow-up to your requests. I regarded the lack of response from your reports to your instructions as a serious failing. A request by a CEO must be understood as a polite order to be performed post-haste. Discussion, debate, and disagreement are healthy up to the point where the CEO says, "O.K., I have heard you, but this is what *I* have decided to do." At this point, all must salute the chief, say, "Yes sir," and bust their asses to make *your* decision work. Remember that a camel is a horse designed by a committee.

"The Boss may not always be right, but the boss is always the Boss."

Post-Script

My loving German great-grandmother used to shake her head (sideways) when she observed one of my teenage faux pas and say, "So bald altes, so spates intelligentes" (So soon old, so late smart). May you glean something useful from these musings and get smart a bit sooner than I did.

Endnotes

1 Stoddard, Samuel (1998-2006). Retrieved June 20, 2010, from Things People Said: *www.rinkworks.com/said/*. Various sources omit the words "can" and/or "just" from this quotation. See, e.g., Ford, P. P. (2002). *The Wit and Wisdom of Yogi Berra*. Illinois: Triumph Books.

2 Livingstone, J. Sterling (January-February 1971). *Myth of the Well-Educated Manager*. Harvard Business Review (President and Fellows of Harvard College).

3 Baker, S. F. (2003). *Sir Francis Bacon: Essays of Francis Bacon, No. 42*. Retrieved June 7, 2010, from The Literature Page: *www.literaturepage.com/read/francis-bacon-essays-86.html/*. Sir Francis Bacon's essays are in the public domain, but references to his essays were retrieved from the foregoing website.

4 For an overview of Peter Drucker's work, including MBO and the social purpose of corporations, see: Drucker, Peter F. (2001). *The Essential Drucker*. New York, NY: HarperCollins Publishers.

5 Retrieved June 7, 2010, from Good Reads: *www.goodreads.com/author/show/11682.ArthurSchopenhauer*.

6 Carr, Nicholas (June 5, 2010). *Does the Internet Make You Dumber?* Retrieved June 21, 2010, from The Wall Street Journal Online: *http://online.wsj.com/article/SB10001424052748704025304575284981644790098.html*.

7 Ibid.

8 Retrieved June 7, 2010, from Brainy Quote: *www.brainyquote.com/quotes/authors/s/satchel_paige.html*.

9 For a thorough history of RPM's growth through acquisitions, see: Dougal, April S., updated by David E. Salamie. *International Directory of Company Histories*. Coypright © 2006 by The Gale Group, Inc. Retrieved July 22, 2010, from Answers.com: *http://www.answers.com/topic/rpm-international-inc-2*.

10 Greiner, Larry E. (July-August 1972, revised ed. May-June 1998). *Evolution and Revolution as Organizations Grow*. Harvard Business Review (President and Fellows of Harvard College).

.